WHOHQ
I0762520

To Steve and Sara Labrecque—EL

For my mom—SK

PENGUIN WORKSHOP
An imprint of Penguin Random House LLC
1745 Broadway, New York, NY 10019
penguinrandomhouse.com

Design by Taylor Abatiell
Text set in Adobe Garamond Pro

The art was created using Adobe Photoshop.

Library of Congress Cataloging-in-Publication Data is available.

First published in the United States of America by Penguin Workshop, 2026

Manufactured in China
HH

ISBN 9798217053582
10 9 8 7 6 5 4 3 2 1

The authorized representative in the EU for product safety and compliance is Penguin Random House Ireland, Morrison Chambers, 32 Nassau Street, Dublin D02 YH68, Ireland, https://eu-contact.penguin.ie.

BRUCE SPRINGSTEEN

A WHO HQ ILLUSTRATED BIOGRAPHY

by
Ellen Labrecque

illustrated by
Sam Kalda

PENGUIN WORKSHOP

A little boy and his mother danced in a modest living room. They twisted to a song by Chubby Checker. The boy and his mom laughed and smiled. One day, this little boy would grow up to sing and dance in front of hundreds of thousands of fans.

WHO WAS THIS YOUNG TWISTER?

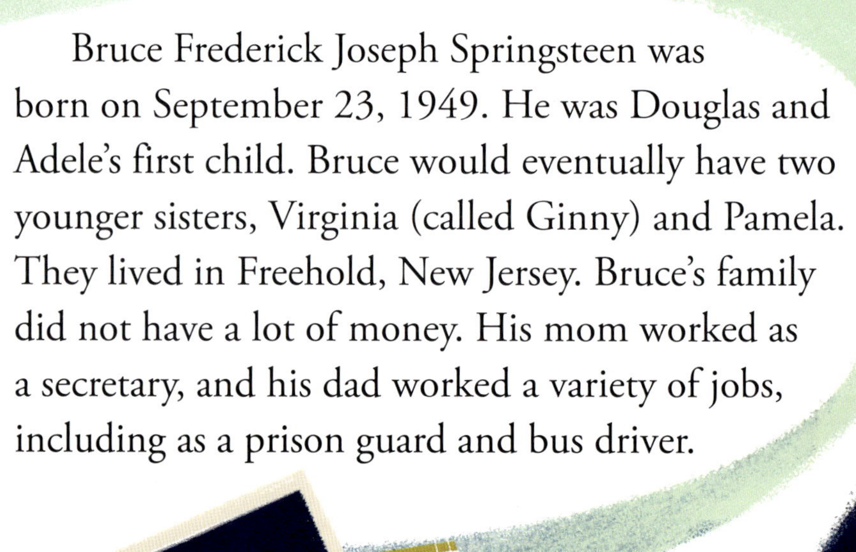

Bruce Frederick Joseph Springsteen was born on September 23, 1949. He was Douglas and Adele's first child. Bruce would eventually have two younger sisters, Virginia (called Ginny) and Pamela. They lived in Freehold, New Jersey. Bruce's family did not have a lot of money. His mom worked as a secretary, and his dad worked a variety of jobs, including as a prison guard and bus driver.

To save money, Bruce and his family lived with his grandparents, Alice and Fred, until he was six years old. Bruce did not have to follow a lot of rules. He sometimes stayed up all night and watched television. “It was upside down, but that was the way it was,” Bruce said.

When Bruce was seven, his family moved to their own apartment three blocks from his grandparents' house. Young Bruce loved to listen to songs from a radio that sat on top of the refrigerator. On the weekends, his family went on rides and listened to music in the car. Bruce especially loved to listen to Elvis Presley. He also watched him perform on television.

When Bruce was fifteen years old, he dragged his mom to a music store in town. It was Christmas Eve 1964, and Bruce wanted an electric guitar. The guitar cost a lot of money—especially for Bruce's family. His mom borrowed money from a bank. The next day, Christmas, he could now rock out all day long.

ELVIS PRESLEY

Elvis Presley was the face of music in the 1950s. His nickname was the King of Rock and Roll.

Elvis was born on January 8, 1935, in Tupelo, Mississippi. Some of his early hits, like "Heartbreak Hotel" and "Hound Dog," made him a superstar singer. Elvis was very handsome and had a deep, melodic voice. He had smooth jet-black hair and wore bold outfits. Elvis was famous for swiveling his hips while dancing onstage. When he performed, the crowd—a lot of whom were teenage girls—screamed in pure joy.

Elvis was Bruce's idol from a young age. He wanted to grow up to be just like him. "Man, when I was nine, I couldn't imagine anyone *not* wanting to be Elvis Presley," Bruce said.

Bruce practiced playing his guitar almost every day. He played in front of a mirror in his bedroom. This way, he could see how his fingers hit the chords. He sometimes practiced as many as six or eight hours a day. “If I wasn’t in school, I was either playing my guitar or listening to records,” Bruce said.

In high school in the 1960s, Bruce joined a band named the Castiles. The name came from a popular soap that teenage kids used at the time. Bruce played lead guitar. The band performed at local teen dances and entered some battle-of-the-bands concerts. Like many young men in the 1960s, Bruce grew his wavy hair long. He wanted to look the part of a rock and roller.

Bruce graduated from Freehold High School in 1967 and took classes at Ocean County College. Bruce felt out of place there, but he did well in one writing class. The teacher recognized Bruce had a way with words. He was a gifted storyteller.

Bruce stopped going to college after a year. Instead, he performed in Asbury Park, New Jersey. The beach town wasn't far from Bruce's hometown of Freehold. One night, Bruce sang at a coffee place called the Upstage Club. Customers in the audience were amazed. "Bruce had this presence," one fan said. "The hairs on the back of your neck would tingle. He had an instinct, a gift."

Other musicians were impressed and wanted to be in a band with Bruce. Together, they formed a band called Child. They performed in Asbury Park and at local colleges. Bruce was the star—the lead singer and guitar player. The band soon changed its name to Steel Mill. They booked larger gigs in places outside of New Jersey, like Virginia and California.

Bruce had a magical quality when he was onstage. He had a husky voice that sang raw and honest lyrics. His concerts were full of energy even when they lasted as long as four hours. He ran all over the stage when he sang and even jumped up on amps and speakers.

In 1972, when he was twenty-three years old, Bruce signed a record contract! This meant Bruce's music would be recorded and sold in stores. His songs would be played on the radio. Bruce formed a new band called Bruce Springsteen and the E Street Band, named after a place in Belmar, New Jersey, where one of the band members lived. Band members started calling Bruce "the Boss" because he was the one in charge. The nickname stuck!

Bruce's first album was called *Greetings from Asbury Park, N.J.* The songs were about life in small-town America, fast cars, and girls. One song was titled "Growin' Up." It was about a teenage boy who didn't follow the rules. Bruce's album received positive reviews, but it didn't sell a lot of copies.

Bruce put out another album ten months after his first one. *The Wild, the Innocent & the E Street Shuffle* didn't sell a lot of copies, either. Bruce knew he needed to come up with a hit song that could play on the radio. Otherwise, the record label wouldn't produce his music anymore. Bruce spent months writing a new song called "Born to Run." The song was about following your dreams.

The song "Born to Run" and the album with the same name were released in August 1975. They were a smash hit. The album sold a lot of copies, and Bruce was featured on the cover of magazines. Bruce and the E Street Band went on tour. They played to sold-out crowds all over the United States, Europe, and Canada! Bruce, now age twenty-six, was truly a rock and roll star!

BRUCE'S ALBUMS

Bruce Springsteen has released 21 studio albums and 121 live albums over his career. He is one of the most successful musical artists in history, selling more than 150 million records worldwide. Here are his top ten bestselling albums ranked by the Recording Industry Association of America.

Born in the U.S.A.
1984

Live 1975–85
1986

Born to Run
1975

Greatest Hits
1995

The River
1980

Darkness on the Edge of Town
1978

Tunnel of Love
1987

Greetings from Asbury Park, N.J.
1973

The Rising
2002

The Wild, the Innocent & the E Street Shuffle
1973

Bruce put out two more successful albums over the next couple of years. He also toured the globe and played in front of bigger crowds. In June 1984, Bruce and his band released the title song and album *Born in the U.S.A.* Bruce was a star before, but this album launched him into the stratosphere! Seven out of the ten singles on the album became top ten hits on *Billboard*'s Hot 100 chart. It was one of the biggest albums of the year.

Bruce's style had evolved since his teenage days. His hair was still shaggy but not as long. He wore a red bandanna around his head, a plain white T-shirt, and old blue jeans. Bruce wanted to look like a working-class hero. His songs told stories about average people doing their best in tough circumstances. Many of his fans could relate to the stories Bruce told. This made him even more popular.

Bruce and the E Street Band toured the world and performed in front of hundreds of thousands of fans. The show's energy felt stronger than a bolt of lightning. Bruce's mom was one of his biggest fans. She attended many of his concerts. Sometimes, Bruce brought her up onstage so she could dance along with him. The location was very different from their days dancing in the living room—but some of the moves were the same!

Bruce's dad was also a fan of his son's music. He had not always been so. Growing up, Bruce had a difficult relationship with his father. Despite this, many of Bruce's songs were inspired by him. "When I was a young man and looking for a voice . . . I chose my father's voice," Bruce said about his dad. "My father was my hero and my greatest foe."

On June 8, 1991, when Bruce was forty-one, he married Patti Scialfa, a singer and guitar player in the band. They eventually had three children together, Evan, Jessica, and Samuel. The family lived in Bruce's home state of New Jersey. This Springsteen house was much bigger and grander than the one from Bruce's childhood.

Shortly after the terrorist attacks of September 11, 2001, Bruce and the E Street Band released a new album called *The Rising*. The music was hopeful and upbeat but also about loss and death. The album reached number one on the *Billboard* 200 chart and sold more than two million copies.

Bruce did not slow down as he got older. In 2009, when Bruce was fifty-nine years old, he and his band performed at halftime of the Super Bowl! Over one hundred million fans watched him on television. In 2017, 2018, and 2021, he performed a one-man show in New York called *Springsteen on Broadway*. Bruce told his life story through his songs.

Throughout his life, Bruce always tried to help people in need. He donated a lot of money to charities for people who did not have enough food to eat. He also tried to help immigrants and veterans who served in the US Armed Forces. He spoke out about social injustices across the world.

Bruce Springsteen has sold more than 150 million albums. He became what he dreamed about as a boy—a rock and roll legend and one of the best songwriters to capture the stories of everyday Americans. In 2023, Bruce and the E Street Band went on tour again. Fans thought it might be Bruce's way of saying farewell. But he said no way!

THE BOSS KNOWS BETTER THAN ANYBODY—
THE SHOW MUST ALWAYS GO ON!

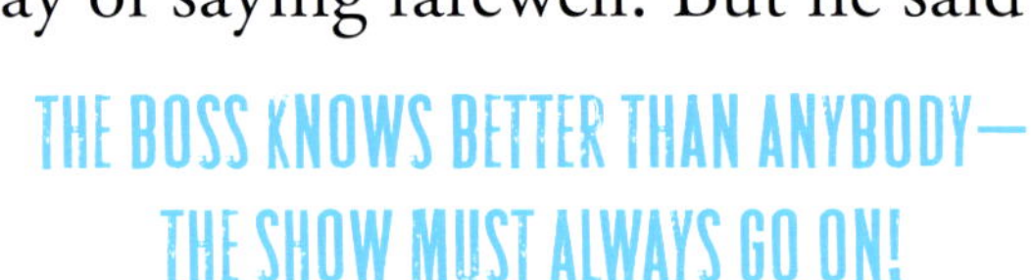

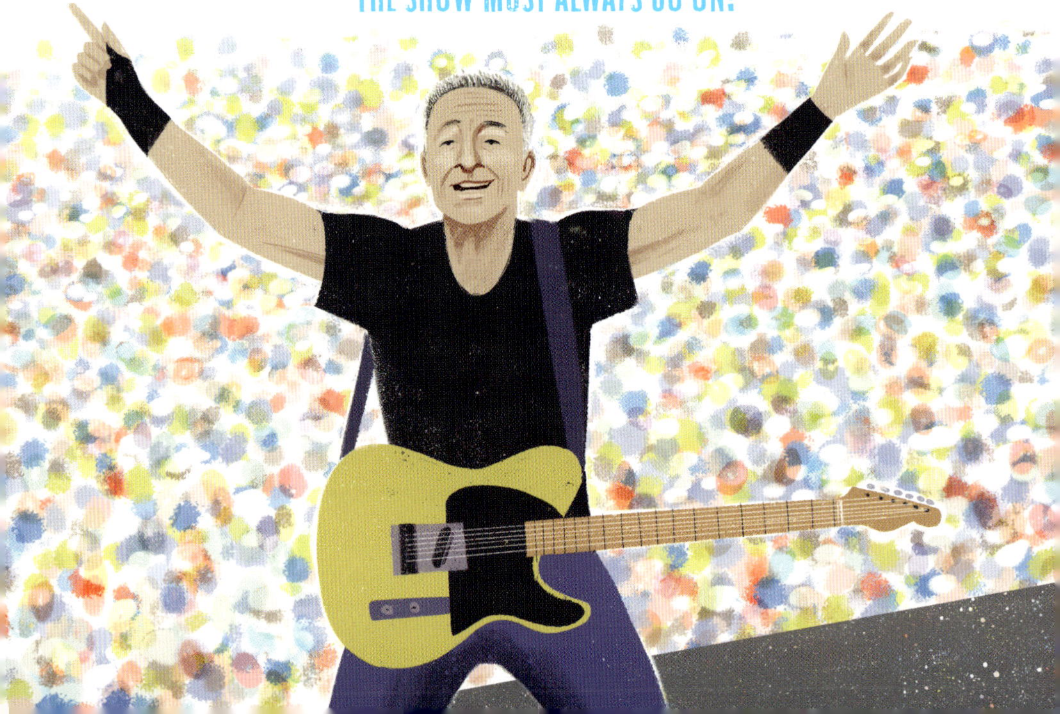

BIBLIOGRAPHY

***Books for young readers**

Carlin, Peter Ames. ***Bruce***. New York: Touchstone, 2012.

Coles, Robert. ***Bruce Springsteen's America: The People Listening, A Poet Singing***. New York: Random House, 2003.

Cullen, Jim. ***Born in the U.S.A.: Bruce Springsteen and the American Tradition***. New York: HarperCollins, 1997.

Marsh, Dave. ***Born to Run: The Bruce Springsteen Story Volume I***. New York: Thunder Mouth's Press, 1996.

Marsh, Dave. ***Glory Days***. New York: Pantheon Books, 1987.

*Sabol, Stephanie. ***Who Is Bruce Springsteen?*** New York: Penguin Workshop, 2016.

Springsteen, Bruce. ***Born to Run***. New York: Simon & Schuster, 2016.

TIMELINE

1949 — Bruce Frederick Joseph Springsteen is born September 23 in Long Branch, New Jersey

1964 — Receives his first electric guitar

1965 — Joins his first band, the Castiles

1973 — *Greetings from Asbury Park, N.J.*, Bruce's first album, is released

1975 — *Born to Run* is released and beloved by fans and critics

1984 — *Born in the U.S.A.* is named the album of the year by *Rolling Stone* magazine

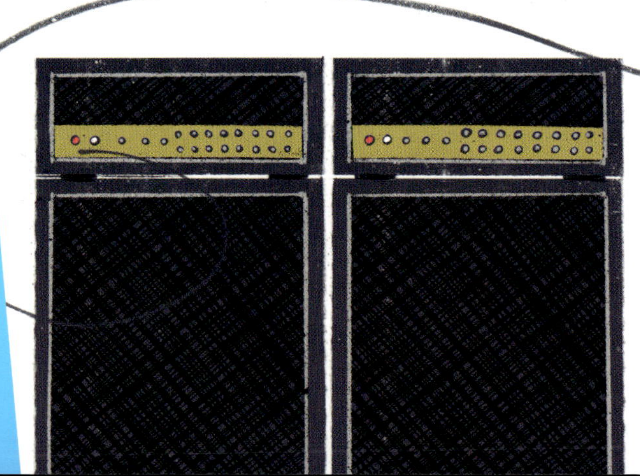

1990 — Bruce and Patti Scialfa's first son, Evan, is born

1991 — Bruce and Patti Scialfa are married

2002 — *The Rising* is released in honor of the victims of the September 11 terrorist attacks on the United States

2009 — Bruce and the E Street Band perform at halftime of the Super Bowl

2017 — Performs the show *Springsteen on Broadway* for the first time

2023 — Bruce and the E Street Band go on tour for the first time in six years

2024 — A documentary about Bruce and the E Street Band, called *Bruce Springsteen: On the Road*, is released

WHOHQ